APRICOT

Apricot

H. Etta

H. Etta

Contents

You cannot give bruised knees as a
present.
There is also no occasion to warrant
the gifting
of scathed elbows.
Here this is, though,
in your hands,
courtesy of my desire to give
simply anything at all.

Do enjoy.

First Printing, 2020

1

Uttered

Deals

I didn't mean it
When I told you
To leave.
I wanted the bad parts
To go to hell
But then all of you
Suddenly disappeared.
And I don't believe that.
That you were all bad.
You were not.
One time you smiled
Instead of sneering.
One time you held my hand

Without breaking my knuckles.
Once you even kissed me
Without biting.
I could see the Angel,
But I suppose the Devil
Knows his kind.
Still,
I would be willing to
Make a deal to have you back.
You loved me so hard
And I miss that.

Enlightened

There is nothing more grounding
Than when you mock my
Spirituality.
You said that if fate is in the stars
You must have the sky in your
Hands.
You prove it to me by
Eating bread at the alter
And in the scissored bend.

Your Nature

Stone-cold but
In a pastel way.
Kind of a bruise but
In a painless way.
Definitely abrasive
But in a gentle way.
Certainly love
Because of
The Way.

With me, Always

Funny how you didn't
Recognize yourself in my home
When there was a book
So full of you
Acting as my coffee table
Centerpiece.

She

Woman with the power.
Woman with the warmth.
Woman.

Professionalism

I know that I am too old
For this,
I should be able to manage
My emotions a bit better
And quit tripping on
The tethers that I draw to
You,
But I feel as a child would
When robbed of their favorite
Blankie.
You feel the same as hot Milo
On a rainy afternoon,
Warm and soothing and
A bit like home.
You cannot hold my hand like
An older sister would their
Little dolly of a human who
Loves them so
And I cannot curl up on your
Lap when the sound
Of loud thunder scares me.
There are rules that exist to quash
My indiscriminate affections
And I do not think that it bothers you
The way that it does me.

That is okay, though.
I still think that you are the best.

Oh Baby

The heathered knit
Stayed draped
Over the back of the chair
For months
After you left.
It was my reminder
That you existed at all.
Even now,
I leave my shoes just far
Enough away
From the entrance
So that there is space
For yours to fit perfectly
Beside them.

A Plea

As if I do not need you!
That was a lie!

A Cuppa?

Each morning,
Soaking up the fading warmth of the half-empty
Teacup
Hoping remnants of our time together
Will appear in the mirage made by the escaped
Loose-leaf mix at the bottom.
They never do.

Little One

I felt so small.
I would have taken the pill,
Drank the potion,
Done anything.

Big One

You are tall like the trees.
I do love that about you,
Even if your shadow
Makes me cold.

Cienna

One sip of Cienna and
I was lost to it.
The memory of you found
My throat,
Slumped at the table of suits,
And restricted my breath.
The taste was of our first day
Together,
Nestled in the margins
Of Lawson,
When Plath had not taught
Me birdsong yet.
How desperate of me
To dare occupy the fantasy of
This ever going well.
Wells was a good start,
Actually,
And I still don't quite know
Where it went wrong,
Which moment was the turning point
For arson,
Because when I burned the paper house
Down I really didn't even think twice.
Bram knows nothing about stoking
As I do.

I have considered that these recollections
Are my attempt at finding a way to blame
You
Instead
As if it wasn't me who pocketed the
Matchbox as soon as I found it
On my morning walk.
It is funny how self-destruction is
An act that is so needy.
Instigated by me,
But projected onto anyone that
Suits it.

Suits,
This table,
Cienna,
You.

If you were to have taught me anything
Before I struck fire upon this castle,
Why could it not have been
How to breathe
Despite the smoke?
My throat is burning from this
Cienna,
From the flames
And you.

Attention

That high-end
Brag that is unsupported
By my lack of drive
To sustain it.
That admiration that I swallow
Because it cannot be reciprocated
Once served.
That inspiration that devours me,
Reflective of my indignation.
The indifference that you behold
When I worship you
As my greatest failure.
That clumsily placed blame
That you do not even know
You are wearing.
The apologies that I write
That you do not realize you
Should be asking for.
This right here,
Another one,
That you will find yourself in.
The way that this is so unwarranted.
The way that I still have so much to say.
The way that you will look for yourself
In everything that I do from here on out, now.

The way that I love that.

Thank You

I found myself
Looking up at you.

Read it again.

I found myself
Looking up at you.

The Poet

Sink my teeth into you
But avoid all the main
Arteries.
It is called
Respect
And mine,
For you?
Crippling.

Sweetie

The arch of your
Back,
The bow in your lips,
The delicate bridging
Of your brows,
The mechanism of your
Knuckles
As your hands bend and
Fold
To hold mine.
I love you
I love you,
Know that.

Do Better

I want to be consumed
By the want and the need
Not the maybe and the might.

Teach Me

Your clinical nature.
Your distance.
Your impression of
A medical practice
Waiting room.
Your 'elevator to the 35th floor
With a stranger'
Imposition.
I imagine you reading this,
With all of your attributes,
Scoffing at the
Lack of substance.
This poem
Doesn't even capture
The tenth of the first
Increment of you,
But it is all I have been given
To work with.

"Young lady finds herself
Perturbed by
The image of a man
That she,
Herself,
Created."

You flounder in the
Abysmal coves
Of my disarrayed head-space
And demand attention
Like some feature-film
Tumbleweed in a ghost town
Long shot.
How unfortunate for me
To never know you
The way that you deserve
To be known.
If I were ever
Given the chance,
I would have pulled
Your brain out
Through your nostrils
Just to devour
Your inner-monologue
Like a Sunday paper,
Interwoven
Your eloquence into
The fabric of my speech
Just to show you
That I had been
Listening.
Alas, you remain contented
In the liminal,

After-office hours
Of our silence
And reaching for
The calculated
Bids of your expression
Will never be an option
For me.
Instead, I can only wonder,
Etch my fingernails
Into the concept of
Who you might be,
Dig deep into the
Flesh of who
I want you to be,
Someone who
Panders and
Ponders and
Pines.
You soft thing,
You dusty paperback,
You cool-toned,
Cool-tempered,
Darling monument
Of a man.
I am desperate to
Capture you
In a still,
Something tangible

That reminds me you
Are real
When you are off
Gallivanting on whims
Of tales that came
Well before you.
You hover in front
Of the lens so indistinctly,
Much like TV static,
And it is hard to grasp
Any idea of you
At all.
To hold you in my hand
Without startling you
And to embrace you
With no warmth?
How?
I can not.
I am in a dispute
With the conundrum
Of your arms-length
Limbo.
I do not know how to
Act,
How to meld myself
To fit against the
Hollows of your
Projected architecture.

It leaves me aimless
And curious;
Anguished and sad.
What to read when
The pages are blank?
Who to know
When there is
No one
Willing to be
Known?

Incentive

Give me something to come back to.

Impact

I certainly miss you.
Like 'a toddler and
A blankie'
Kind of
Miss you
And there is no
Need for that amount
Of missing to be
Occupying the spaces
In my chest
But it is still
Very much there.
The missing.
The empty.
The nothingness.
The
'No you',
So full
And big
And unable to be
Ignored.

The Other Side

Maybe I am just bitter,
But it does not seem much
Greener, anyway.

2

Sir

Tide

I curled up in the undercurrents
Of your joke to
Bathe in the truth of it.
You want me,
Don't you?

Two of Us

The seasons change
But I don't
And that's what you like
Babe,
Isn't it?
Tell them how I love you
The way that gravity exists.
So consuming,
So involved in it all,
So much.
I'm a center point,
I'm a home base,
I'm the docked ship
That you are anchored to.
You are safe with me.
You are.
I am where you belong.
I am.

Insistence

An impression,
I yearned
To make a good one
On you.
I plucked the Forget-Me-Not flowers
And breathed them in
So hard that the pollen
Became wedged in my nostrils.
Every inhalation was a sneeze-inducing
Reminder that I needed to become something
Profound enough
To have you recall the memory of me
In each instance where it was most
Inappropriate.
I wore the lace,
Spoke that way,
Plumped up my lips.
The will to survive in your mind
Became a personality trait
And it shaped me
Into the girl you know now.
The desperate one,
With sticky hands that clutch
At your spine
To stop your mind from running

Away from me.
All that I am
Is because of you
So I have to remember,
If you ever leave,
That it is of no fault
Of my own,
Because I am
All that you could have
Ever asked for,
Even if you never asked
For me in the first place.

Storm Warning

Last I heard
You were begging for me,
The ground became you
And the rise of the tide
Was your desperate inhale
Before the next
Scream of my name.
I walked until my shadow
Lost the sun,
Missed your eruptions
By miles and smiled
When they were announced on
The news.
I am so much higher,
So much drier,
And you are just some downtrodden
Thing
Strewn along the East Coast.
How wonderful it is
To have avoided
Your disaster.

ICT

Topless under the livewires
Because the thrill is worth it,
I suppose.
It has been a long month
Of short circuits and near
Electrocutions,
Yet I am still here,
Wetting you down
Like some animalistic freak
With a death wish.
As if this contact will mend
The heart of you.
As if this sweat,
This spit,
This cum
Will fix what needs intervention.
The man on the helpline asked,
"Have you tried turning it off
And back on again?"
Yes. All too much.
That is my exact problem.

Dine in or Take Away?

He licks his fingers dry
And then slurps like a leech would
While I lay oiled and stuffed
As a roast.
This fast-food business doesn't pay me enough
To feel good about being dubbed
A Thanksgiving turkey.
He's the only one that's thankful.

Human

Belly-up like a squashed bug.
I had heard the stories
But I never believed them.
Then it was me,
On bitumen that was scorching,
Burning in the sun that I
Had once worshipped.
How can one understand it
Without having experienced it?
I was no Icarius,
I knew where to stop,
Yet I still disintegrated.
Now I want to tell Helios
To forget I ever attempted
Such an ambitious endeavor,
Because I was so close to meeting with him
On his east-bound journey
But I am so obviously not worthy.
Trying is a sorry act.
Shame is forever.
My lesson has been learned.

Valentine

Cup the face of the sweet talker
Whose teeth do not rot.
Kiss them.

Theft

Pick your pockets
For some change
To reflect the sun that is
Shining in mine.
Aim the beam into
Your stormy night and
You will feel so much lighter.

Appease

You gave me so much
Of what I
Never asked for
But I still
Said thank you.
So, I think I am
Just as bad.

Big Man

Your essence of bravado
Lives under your top hat
And it comes out at every party.
You are some small-town,
Unfulfilled showstopper,
Some magician with a cape
From a costume shop that is
Just two blocks to the left
For those trying so hard
To be right.
Cheap gimmicks will
Never be enough for them,
But what else is there?
I applaud you for doing anything
At all
In the bounds of a village
That has no room for you.

Let's Talk About That

I gave a one-trick show pony
A tip at the bar and he fed me cheap
Shots all night.
These men like to laugh with rotten teeth,
Like to watch with wandering eyes,
Like to feel with rough hands,
But I am rough, too
And when he said,
"Don't patronize me, *sweetheart*,"
I told him to go fuck himself
With the same bottle of bourbon
That already fucked his family.

Entirety

Something of anything
And
Anything of something.
That is not all that there is
And I will not accept it
From you.

Good News

I am not sure that I need you
Like I first thought.

3

Feline

Vengeance

Found you grappling
At the edges of some
Long-gone
Ghost.
You said you went for tea
With them,
Let them take off your
Coat,
Let their spine lean
Flush against the wall
Of the hallway.
At least you were honest.
Now I can see why they are seemingly

Void of flesh and bone and conscience.
You pocketed the
Memory of them so fast,
Left them hollow and pining and desperate.
I find it to be no surprise
That they let you in
As soon as you unlatched the
Door to our living room.
I would have spread myself
Apart just the same,
Would have begged to be filled
By you again if you had ever
Left me to the dust and
Buried me deep
The way
That you did them.
I spoke with her after you did it.
Met her in the morgue with half of
My soul left and no sanity
To be found.
It all made sense then,
She kissed me and I could taste
No trace of guilt on her lips.
Your mother raised a
Bastard because she
Was married to one,
And now all of these
Girls are sick

And dead
And dying
Because of you.
I wrote you a letter before I left.
To you, it was one of heartbreak
And pity,
But I penned it as a
Respectful
'Go fuck yourself'.

You can
Find us all at the graveyard
Plaiting hair and devouring fruit,
Nourishing ourselves after
Your ill-treatment.
You have created a society of
Women who know now
How to haunt,
Who find you
Right when you think
You have settled
And steal the
One who intends on
Bearing your life-instilled
Seed.
There will be no more you,
In any form,
Ever.
Your ghosts are their

Guardian Angels.
Our division grows
Each time that you fuck up.
You are despised.

Still Here

Under my nails,
On my lips,
In the silence of my morning
Meditation.
You are there
And I am smiling.

Too Late, but Only For Now

I had dog-eared the corners
So that I could come back to her,
But when I returned
Her name read differently and
Her placement in the chapter was off.
I asked the fill character if something
Had happened in my absence,
But they just shook their head
Before hurrying off to their next
Feature.
Her voice found me on page 102.
"Can you meet me?"
She was burrowed in a block of intense
Dialogue on 250 by the time I had caught up.
We were in a coffee shop, in the corner,
And the man beside her was eyeing me
Warily.
She was so invested in the conversation
That she almost missed me standing there.
"Oh," was all she said.
She nervously brushed the hair
From her shoulder.
The necklace that I had given her
On 68
Was no longer around her neck and

Her nails were painted a rosy pink
Instead of the red
That she had always preferred.
"Can we help you?"
The man beside her asked.
He seemed frustrated,
Had a hand outstretched protectively
To hold around her wrist
As if she were a child
Incapable of avoiding strangers.
I wasn't a stranger, though.
She and I both knew that
And so did her body when it almost
Stood to embrace me.
The man clenched his hand
A little tighter
And her desperate stare compensated
For her lack of a greeting.
"Sorry for the disruption," I stepped back.
She was watching me, still.
I was watching her.
She gave a small smile, a sorry one.
I gave her nod.
We had been on different pages before
But we would find each other again.
We always did.

Home

It is the season for the culling of the weed
That has consumed this land for too long.
Beginning with the outskirts and cornering
The last remnants of it in the heart of the field,
There will be a burning of the dead-weight
Once pulled
And a ritual commemorating the new life
That can now flourish.
Watch as the seedlings of closure rise
In place of what was once killing you
And the sky rains with pride
To nourish them.
Dig your roots in, now.
You are safe here,
I promise.

Underbelly

Nail polish with a purple hue
Scratched up on the inside
Of you,
Under a pine slab
In your cousin's house.
Table for two.

Golden

Honeycomb hair pulled back
And a citrine rock
On her finger.
Have you ever met
Sunshine before?

Good Morning

Crouching at the base of the willow
At 4am.
Ten pushes and baby was out,
Slippery like the local coral fish
And squawking far too loud.
Baby told stories about the womb
Through her cries
And we all listened politely.
I would have given up dawn forever
If it meant that I could stay sitting in her dusk.

P is for Patronize

Penny pulls a park
Close to Prim
But lets the Prius
To her left
Act as a divider.
"Fuck you,"
Prim mouths through
The four glass
Panes
Between them.
Penny smiles.

The letter 'P',
Puh, Puh, Puh,
Is for Patronize.

Childhood

There is no handbook
For a broken bond
Like ours.
I am still tethered to you
By years of memories
And it feels as though I am
Ripping the teeth from
My mouth
Then bleeding out
On some lonely,
Back-alley pavement.
My knees are
Just as collapsed
As the bridge
Right now.
Still, I must do this,
Because being your favorite dolly
Is breaking my heart.
We are big girls, so,
Tell your mother
That my mother said
That I am too busy to talk
The next time that you call
To speak with me,
Okay?

Sirens

You were too temporary,
Too unfixed.
I could grab you
By the collar of your dress
To make you stay
But you would just slip it right off
And leave anyway.
And how does one deal with that?
The deciduous nature of you
Could send me off the deep end
And then you would be watching me drown
Again,
Smiling the way that you do
When weak girls dip their toes in
And attach themselves to your allure.
I die in both versions of this story.
I'm either inundated
With too much of you
Or withering away in your absence
And there seems to be no winning
Balance.
I always find myself marveling
At your absolute gall.
You should know that I love you still,
Despite it all.

Love it is while I'm cracked open
On a moss-covered bank.
Love it is when I'm in a ditch
On the ocean floor
Being scratched and scathed by the
Deposited shucked shells
That once held my hopes
For us.
You've gutted me just the same,
You have.
I scream your name by the oceanside
And ache with a salt-dried throat
Just to hear you once more.
They do not tell you
That the silence of a siren
Is deafening.
They do not tell you
That it is not just the sailors
Who have so far to fall.
It is me,
Only a girl,
Who is also begging on all fours.
Because I swear I need you.

Morning Walks with Her

It was me who was breathing
In your perfume in gasps of laughter
As the wind cradled you and then
Flew back to meet me.
Hints of every good thing.
Now you wear
A different scent
And I take the train,

Sucker

We took the suckers
And stuck them
Onto the underside of the
Bed frame.
My room smelled
Like caramel candies
For the rest of the summer
Until Ainsley scraped
Them all off.
I had this blister on
My heel
For the three weeks
That we were together,
And now the spot
Is like new again,
Is devoid of the
Remnants of our adventures.

The tree outside my window
Got cut down.

Mangoes are no longer
In season so the café
Down the street stopped
Selling Tropical Storms,

I tried making one at home
With a mango that we had
Kept frozen
But it wasn't the same.
I think I left out a dash
Of vanilla essence.
I'm not sure.
The blanket fort in the
Backyard
Got sodden with the
Morning mildew.
I had been sleeping in it
Until it became so wet
That I couldn't.
Dad told me to come inside
To sleep,
Or else I would get sick.
I tried writing you letters,
Like we said we would,
But I lost the scrap of cardboard
That had your new postal address
Written on it.
What I wanted to write to you,
What I wanted to say,
Is that winter feels bad this year.
There is no longer any trace of
Sunshine,
Summer,

Or you, Sarah,
And that scares me.
I don't know how to be in this cold
Without any warmth,
How to survive without
A twin flame.
Maybe you've still got
My address on that napkin
And you'll write to me,
Instead.
I'll go and check the mail again now.

4

Nettles

I Miss Myself Most

They said that my poetry
Should tell a story
But I do not have
One.
It is in shambles
From you;
Starts officially on page ten
After nine pages of uncertainty,
Then ends on twelve
Just to pick up on fourteen
After two tear-stained
Blank
Pages.

I am missing whole chapters.
Some are in a language
That I cannot remember
How to read.
You creased the pages you
Liked,
Dog-eared them
Just to never return.
Fuck you
For that.
I have nothing to show
For myself
Because of you.
Not even you.
Not even me.

The Truth

You could have held me
And we could have danced
And I could have saved
Those tears
And they could have
Stared, unsure,
And we could have laughed,
So certain,
And pigs could have flown
But they didn't
And it didn't have to
End like this
But it did
And you're not to blame
But you so are
And I tell everyone
I'm not bitter
But I am
But you know that
Because it is you
Who made me like
This
And you won't admit that
But you don't need to
Because I know.

I know.

Wrong Side

Each crease in the bedsheet
Is a bad dream.
My sweaty palms
Grapple at them
As if a tightened fist will
Squeeze them into
Non-existence
Rather than keeping them
Ever-present
As they always
Are.
Is it any wonder I wake
So tired?
Sleep is where
The hauntings take place.
I am exhausted from this rest.

Fever Dream

We're in a field
And there are monsters
Chasing us.
I lose sight of you
But can hear your feet
Thudding on the dirt still.
I hear them until I don't.
I can't figure out which one
Of us is dead.

Energy

I felt you
With me there.
You were a part of the
Furniture,
In the hardwood,
Lingering like the stains
On a piss-soaked sheet.
It is not enough to scream
At you to leave.
You would never do that,
Would you?
You bust each time I wake up
Crying at night.
You are a real sick fuck,
Aren't you?

Escape

Pack your bags.
I have decided that somewhere
Else is where I would like to be.
We will leave around midnight
So that the highway is not so convoluted
And I will play the music that we would
Dance to as kids.
Our snacks will be whatever we can scrounge
From our parents' kitchen and
We will laugh as if our memories of the past
Do not exist.
This will be fun.
I swear it will be fun.
Just pack your bags.

Frost Bite

I made a fire in our woods
And burned half of Jackson
Down
Because I thought that
You were coming back.
The season of you
Lasted so long that
I had forgotten coats should
Not be worn in
Summer heat.
I wore them anyway.
I cannot walk straight
On black ice
Or see clearly in a blizzard.
I cannot be with you
Without being lost.

Please please please,
Stay gone.

Dead-end

I have screamed your name
Into glass jars and kept them stowed
In the cabinet
For the days when I forget
What your impact sounds like.
This morning I unscrewed one of the lids
Just to hear the same thing as each time before.
It sounded like desperation and
Agony and please don't leave me
And why don't you care and what
Can I do to be enough?
It sounded redundant.
It sounded like I should know
Better by now
Than to have the nerve to
Still miss you.
It sounded like I still don't.

The Pulp

There are moments when you
Flash
In the forefront of my thoughts
And you seem just as you were
Before.
It is so easy to hate you on paper
But, when you stand right there
In my mind like that,
Looking,
Being,
Like that,
I can no longer pinpoint my reasons
Although there are
So many.
To remind myself,
I climb the rungs
Of your ribs
And use your twisted mind
As a lookout.
I see the carked fruits in the
Barren
Fields, the fruits you suckled
Until you were sick,
Their final sprouts of citrus
Seeping out like a last breath.

They hold no blame for you
Yet they lay rotting because of
You,
You with your teeth lined with
The kernels of the
Disheveled pomegranate,
You with your gums coated
In the busted pips
Of the mandarin.
You are one very sweet monster
And I am still learning how
To be afraid
Because when you flash
Like that
In the main street of my mind
And you seem,
Feel,
Just like that
Reality contorts in your favor
And I am back to being
The apricot that begs
For pitting.
You would get drunk on the ferment,
And I would feel proud that
I had anything to offer you
At all.
I should just tell you to
Bite me

But the insult would get lost
In the desire
To have you pining for me
Once more,
Never-mind the fact that you would
Milk me dry
And revel in the loss
Of my entirety.

Confessional

Feeling like I miss you
Despite
The wine having spilled
From our cup
One too many
Times.

Feeling comforted by the
Red stains on the
Dress that I wore
The last time our
Togetherness
Got us drunk.

Feeling displaced
At the dry cleaners.

Feeling the worst
In my
Sunday best, now.

Feeling like you are
Right there
As I take communion,
Wet my lips with

Holy memories.

Feeling like the body
Of Christ
Was mangled with mine
On the 26th floor
That one July.

Feeling like religion
Finds you
In the weirdest ways.

Feeling like
Excommunication
Feels like
Death.

Feeling like there's
No afterlife
Unless you are
In it
With me.

Feeling like
I never should have
Believed
In the first place.

Natural Selection

I love you so much
That it makes me sick.
The peat of my lining
Wants nothing to do with you,
Tries to expel you like
A bug,
But I just fucking love your colors.

My Love

I would have followed you
If you hadn't removed me
Like a layer of dead skin
So heavy that it made your feet drag.
I am no shapeshifter like you,
Can't change in the night
For the sake of convenience,
Or drop someone on their head
After kissing their face the
Whole day prior.
I put that on my Christmas list, though.
To be more like you.
Because I have learned so much
From being me
And I know that you cannot
Keep running from yourself.
If I am more like you,
It means that it will be us,
Together forever,
Just as I had hoped.
Would that not be
Grand?

If You Were a Bottle of Pasta Sauce

The callout requested
A clean-up on aisle four
And I cursed out the staff who
Threatened my spill with
Their equipment.
I had you this whole time,
Bottled so safely and sealed
In so tight
And yet you still escaped me
In a shattering blitz of finality.
I couldn't tell who was most
Damaged.
You hit the ground hard
But your shards
Cut me deep
And together we were just lamely pooling
On the tiles of the grocery store.
If I wasn't so invested in the pain
Of no longer having you
I would have been embarrassed
To see our story on the front page
Of the local a week later.
Admittedly, it felt nice to see
That we wouldn't be forgotten
Because, even now, I don't think

I have the strength to properly
Speak of you
Without
Falling off of the shelf
Myself.

Roadkill

They say the damage control
Was so swift
And effective
That they barely noticed
My blood on the
Bitumen at all.

Favorite Person

It is not that you are special.
It is that I am too kind.

False Witness

Hands clasped.
Head bowed.
Eyes shut.
Jesus, if you're there,
Give me a sign.
Jaw clenched.
Legs stiff.
Heart pounding.
Jesus, if you're there,
Speak louder.
Fingers shaking.
Brow sweating.
Stomach knotted.
Jesus, if you're there,
I don't believe you.
Faith lost.
Faith lost.
Faith lost.
Jesus, if you're there,
I wish you were.

To be Framed

A pool of pixel-ink
Emerges on the screen
As I type to a crescendo
In your name.
You do not deserve
Poetry,
But the young girl in me
Asked nicely
And I am nothing
If not kind
To her, at least.
The flesh of the
Stanza laces 'You'
As a concept into
'Romance'
As a theme,
And I gag at the
Pace of the waltz.
I wonder how it
Feels for you
To be seeing yourself
Splayed on a page
Like this.
I have you pinned
Like a monarch on

Styrofoam
And soon I will
Display you in
The back room
As some sad, nearly forgotten
Memory.

A pastime.

You miserable creature.
My poor little reason for
Rhyme.
Denounced
From Everything
To only Something,
One tiny frame in
A gallery of
All that is
More significant.
Watch as the fluorescence
Bears the truth
Of what this love
Meant to you.
Watch as I
Make a monument
Out of the man who comes
After.
Watch as a child would

Their mother
When she roars with a
Fed-up fury.
I am done now.
For absolute good.

5

Heaven

THERE ISN'T ONE.

Lightning Source UK Ltd.
Milton Keynes UK
UKHW010635250121
377629UK00003B/704